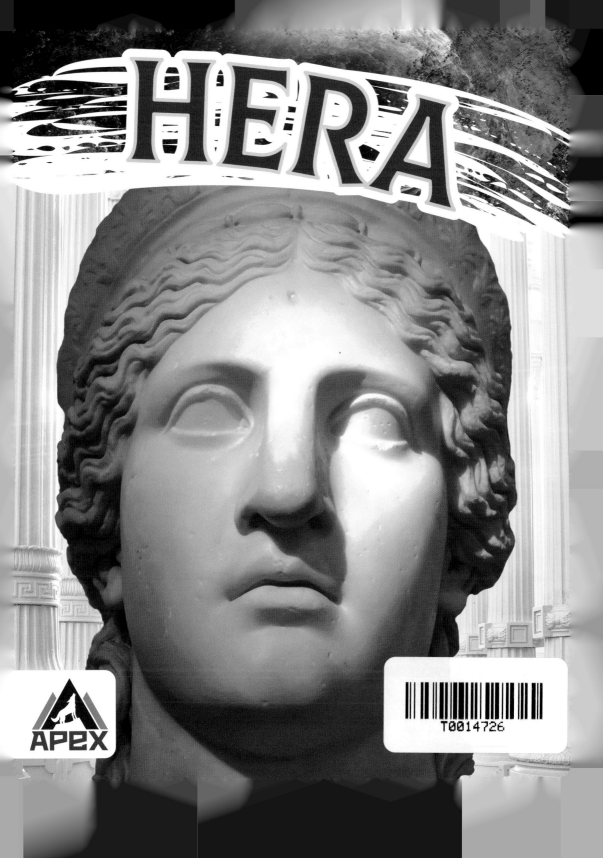

HERA

WWW.APEXEDITIONS.COM

Apex is distributed by North Star Editions:
sales@northstareditions.com | 888-417-0195

Produced for Apex by Red Line Editorial.

Photographs ©: Shutterstock Images, cover, 1, 4–5, 6–7, 7, 8–9, 12–13, 14–15, 16–17, 18–19, 20–21, 22–23, 24–25, 26, 27, 29; iStockphoto, 10–11

Library of Congress Control Number: 2020952912

ISBN
978-1-63738-015-4 (hardcover)
978-1-63738-051-2 (paperback)
978-1-63738-121-2 (ebook pdf)
978-1-63738-087-1 (hosted ebook)

Printed in the United States of America
Mankato, MN
082021

NOTE TO PARENTS AND EDUCATORS

Apex books are designed to build literacy skills in striving readers. Exciting, high-interest content attracts and holds readers' attention. The text is carefully leveled to allow students to achieve success quickly. Additional features, such as bolded glossary words for difficult terms, help build comprehension.

TABLE OF CONTENTS

UNLUCKY ECHO

Hera was searching for her husband, the god Zeus. He had gone missing again. Hera went to Earth to look for him.

Hera ruled the lives of women. She was married to Zeus, the king of the gods.

Nymphs are connected to parts of nature, such as mountains and rivers.

Suddenly, a **nymph** blocked Hera's way. Her name was Echo. Hera tried to go around her. But Echo wouldn't let Hera go. She kept asking Hera questions.

Greek gods sometimes came to Earth in disguise. Zeus became an animal. Hera turned into an old woman.

In one story, Zeus turned into a swan.

Zeus was the Greek god
of thunder and lightning.

Hera got angry. She cursed Echo. From then on, Echo could only repeat what others said. Then Hera stomped off to keep looking for Zeus.

HERA'S CHILDREN

Hera and Zeus had several children. One was Ares, the god of war. Hebe was another. She was the goddess of youth.

QUEEN OF THE GODS

Hera was the queen of the Greek gods. She was also the goddess of marriage and family.

Hera ruled with Zeus from Mount Olympus. They're often shown seated on thrones.

Hera was powerful and smart. But she was also **vain**. As a result, she could be jealous and **vengeful**.

Hera often wore a crown. Sometimes, she carried a scepter.

In one story, Hera fought other goddesses over a golden apple.

Hephaestus was the god of fire and metalworking.

For example, one woman claimed she was as beautiful as Hera. Hera turned her into a stork.

FAMILY DRAMA

Hera did not get along with her son Hephaestus. She threw him off Mount Olympus. To get back at her, he made a beautiful throne. It trapped Hera when she sat on it.

Hera's sacred animals were the peacock and the cow. They often appear with her in art.

HERA AND ZEUS

Zeus was not a faithful husband. He had many lovers. Hera disliked them and their children. She often tried to hurt them.

Hercules was the son of Zeus and a human. Hera tried to have monsters kill him.

In one story, Zeus fell in love with Io. Zeus turned Io into a cow to hide her from Hera. But his trick didn't work. Hera found the cow. She sent a giant to guard it.

Hera sometimes sent snakes or dragons to attack people she disliked.

Hera sent Argus to keep Zeus away from Io. This giant had eyes all over his body.

After Argus died, Hera moved his eyes to the tail of a peacock.

Zeus sent the god Hermes to kill the giant. In response, Hera sent a fly. It chased Io away.

A FIERY TRICK

Once, Zeus loved a human named Semele. Hera tricked them. She got Zeus to show Semele his true form. Seeing it made Semele burst into flames.

HONORING HERA

Many Greek women prayed to Hera. Some prayed about their families or marriages. Others asked for help having babies.

In Rome, Hera was known as Juno. She was said to guard the whole Roman Empire.

Across Greece, festivals were held to honor Hera. One took place in Olympia. It was a sports festival for female athletes. Girls ran races.

The Temple of Hera in Olympia is one of the oldest temples in Greece.

SPORTS IN GREECE

Olympia held a sports festival for Zeus, too. It was called the Olympics. For a while, only men could **compete**. But women sometimes owned the horses or **chariots** they used.

Hera was also the **guardian** of two cities. Their names were Argos and Samos. Hera protected them.

Ruins of Hera's temple still stand in Samos today.

Pomegranate trees have grown in Greece since ancient times.

Hera is sometimes shown holding a pomegranate. In ancient Greece, this fruit was a **symbol of fertility**.

COMPREHENSION QUESTIONS

Write your answers on a separate piece of paper.

1. Write a few sentences explaining the main ideas of Chapter 2.

2. Do you think it was fair for Hera to attack Zeus's children? Why or why not?

3. Which animal was sacred to Hera?

    A. the fly

    B. the peacock

    C. the stork

4. Why would Zeus not want Hera to find Io?

    A. Io would make Hera go away.

    B. Io would like Hera more than him.

    C. Hera would probably try to hurt Io.

5. What does **faithful** mean in this book?

*Zeus was not a **faithful** husband. He had many lovers.*

> **A.** staying true to one person or idea
> **B.** being hard to trust or rely on
> **C.** being a bad example to others

6. What does **athletes** mean in this book?

*It was a sports festival for female **athletes**. Girls ran races.*

> **A.** people who start a fire
> **B.** people who rule a country
> **C.** people who do a sport

Answer key on page 32.

GLOSSARY

chariots
Two-wheeled carts pulled by horses or other animals.

compete
To try to beat others in a game or event.

fertility
The ability to have babies.

guardian
A person who protects something or someone.

nymph
A beautiful spirit that lives in trees, water, or other parts of nature.

sacred
Having close ties to a god, goddess, or religion.

scepter
A staff held by a ruler as a symbol of power.

symbol
An object or idea that stands for and reminds people of something else.

vain
Caring a lot about how you look.

vengeful
Wanting to hurt someone who has hurt you.

TO LEARN MORE

BOOKS

Flynn, Sarah Wassner. *Greek Mythology*. Washington, DC: National Geographic, 2018.

Gagne, Tammy. *Hera: Queen of the Greek Gods*. North Mankato, MN: Capstone Press, 2019.

Temple, Teri. *Hera: Queen of the Gods, Goddess of Marriage*. Mankato, MN: The Child's World, 2019.

ONLINE RESOURCES

Visit **www.apexeditions.com** to find links and resources related to this title.

ABOUT THE AUTHOR

Christine Ha lives in Minnesota. She enjoys reading and learning about myths and legends from around the world.

INDEX

Answer Key:
1. Answers will vary; **2.** Answers will vary; **3.** B; **4.** C; **5.** A; **6.** C